201 MORE
HANDY HINTS FOR
HORSE PERSONS

KAREN BUSH

Illustrated by Claire Colvin

KENILWORTH PRESS

Copyright © 1999 Karen Bush
Illustrations © Claire Colvin

First published in the UK in 1999
by Kenilworth Press, an imprint of Quiller Publishing Ltd

Reprinted 2002, 2007

British Library Cataloguing-in-Publication Data
A catalogue record for this book is available from
the British Library

ISBN 978 1 872119 12 0

Printed in China

Kenilworth Press
An imprint of Quiller Publishing Ltd
Wykey House, Wykey, Shrewsbury, SY4 1JA
tel: 01939 261616   fax: 01939 261606
email: info@quillerbooks.com
website: www.kenilworthpress.co.uk

Introduction

The horse world has seen huge changes since the publication of the first volume of *201 Handy Hints for Horse Persons*. Ideas and products still at a fledgling stage when it was originally written, and only just beginning to make an impact, are now very much commonplace in the stable yard – from Velcro fastenings, synthetic rugs, boots and saddlery, to new feedstuffs, bitting and bedding systems to name just a few. Not only is there a whole new range of products based on modern technology and research, but also the choice is wider than ever before – horses never had it so good.

There are some things, however, that never change: riding and horse keeping is still on the increase, and whether you own, share or loan a horse or pony it remains an expensive and time-consuming hobby. This book continues where the first left off, with ideas to help make bills a little cheaper, the chores a little easier and the time you spend with your horse generally more pleasant and stress-free. You will find that it also takes into account the appearance of new products which can often be employed in ways the manufacturers hadn't perhaps originally intended – such as those tubs of feed supplements, which when empty can be so useful for safely storing odds and ends!

Finally, do remember that although there are many ways in which you can save both time and money, you should never consider economising on those things essential to your horse's well-being, such as correct feeding, regular worming, shoeing and veterinary attention, and never compromise the safety of either yourself or your horse.

A small ramp fitted to a trough allows small birds and animals to escape if they get into the water.

4

1

Finding small dead birds and animals floating in the water-trough is not only unpleasant but also contaminates the water and may put horses off drinking. Place a small ramp from the water to the lip of the trough to enable them to escape.

2

Encouraged by a thriving market for secondhand horse clothing, some thieves will stop at nothing, and have even been known to strip the rugs off horses standing in fields during broad daylight. Take preventive measures against this happening by painting your name or postcode on rugs: make sure you use an indelible product which won't damage the fabric – check with the manufacturer if you aren't sure. Paint your postcode on the roof and side of your trailer too, as this will make it easier to identify and trace if it is stolen.

3

A large part of staying warm in winter is keeping the wet and the wind out – invest in a pair of waterproof overtrousers that will do this. In addition, they will ensure that when carrying full buckets of water, you don't end up slopping any of it inside your wellington boots.

4

Don't throw away old towels no longer fit for use around the house – save them for jobs around the yard such as drying off a wet horse, tack cleaning, or for use as stable rubbers.

5

If you need to restrict your horse's access to grazing to prevent him from becoming overweight, rather than condemning him to being kept stabled for long periods, which can lead to boredom, over-freshness and stable vices, look into other solutions instead. Portable electric fencing can be used to reduce the grazing area, or you could introduce sheep, which will graze the grass back very short. If neither of these options is feasible, use a bucket muzzle with a mesh bottom which will limit the amount of grass he can reach to eat, whilst still allowing him to drink freely.

6

Use a hand-held power-wash at car service stations to help remove ingrained dirt and grime from turn-out rugs – it's quicker, easier and more effective than scrubbing by hand. Transport wet rugs home in a sturdy plastic bag or plastic bin. **Tip:** Make sure the rug is thoroughly rinsed of any suds.

7

Duvet-style rug liners are very popular nowadays, being light but very warm: they are also expensive to buy. You can easily make one instead for a fraction of the price: buy a double or king-sized one from a market or secondhand sale – they are easy to cut to fit and to sew, adding Velcro for the breast fastenings. **Tip:** Buy the hollow fibre type of duvet, not the down variety.

8

Neck covers are often a better buy than hoods – horses rarely object to them being put on or taken off, they tear less easily and if they slip they won't interfere with the vision. You can easily make your own from old rug materials.

Neck covers can be made quite easily from old rug materials.

9

Shell suits bought cheaply at secondhand sales make great coveralls if you want to keep your clothes clean whilst doing messy chores such as mucking out and clipping – and you won't overheat in them in warmer weather. You can even hack to shows wearing them over the top of your show clothes so you arrive still looking spotless: and as they are usually brightly coloured they'll also help make you more visible to other road users on the way there.

10

If you buy a rug which has unusual fastenings, buy spares from the manufacturer in case a part breaks, otherwise you may have a long wait if the saddler has none in stock and needs to order them in specially. If the job is urgent it might also lead to a bigger repair bill if different fastenings have to be used instead. **Tip:** If you have rugs with breast fastenings that consist of straps which thread through slots, keep spares of these too, as they often become detached and lost when wet and hung up to dry.

11

A quick, cheap and easy way of hanging wet turn-out rugs up to dry is to hammer two sturdy nails into your tackroom wall: then hang the rug from them by the metal D's at the back to which the leg straps are clipped. If your rug doesn't use leg straps, it takes only a few minutes to sew on metal D-rings for this purpose.

12

If you are unsure as to whether your horse's diet is correct, most feed manufacturers now employ nutritionists and have telephone help-lines which you can call for free advice.

13

Dustbins can make useful feed storage containers, but sometimes larger rodents learn to push the lids off to get to their contents. Prevent this from happening by hooking a bungee strap onto one side handle, looping it through the lid handle and then hooking the other end to the opposite dustbin side handle. If you suspect that someone at your yard is pilfering your feed, use a chain with a padlock attached instead.

14

Metal male/female rug fastenings can have an annoying habit of popping undone. Slip a small rubber O-ring or elastic band over the neck of the metal T-bar-shaped fitting before doing it up, as this will reduce the amount of play and the likelihood of it accidentally coming undone.

Make your rug fastenings more secure with a small elastic band.

15

Old chest-freezers that no longer work can be kept or bought cheaply and used as vermin-proof rug- or feed-storage chests.

16

Buy plain jump poles as they are cheaper than painted ones. Jazz them up yourself by using paint left over from home decorating jobs. **Tip:** Painting poles is made easier if you hammer a six-inch nail into each end and then hang them between two trestles or jump stands.

17

Buy a few lengths of ribbon which you can use to plait over the top of your bridle browband for shows. It is cheaper than buying a ready-made one and you will also be able to get the exact colour combinations you want, and can change them whenever you wish. **Tip:** When competing in showing classes, check that it is correct to use a coloured browband, rather than a plain one.

18

Don't throw away damaged old rugs which aren't worth repairing. Any fabric you don't want to keep for repair patches on other rugs can be used to make your own saddle protectors, tail guards and even travel boots. Don't throw away old fleece jackets either, as they can be cut down to make girth sleeves.

19

Disposable nappies can make useful dressings beneath bandages, tending to draw discharge away from wounds and keep them dry; and they are cheaper to buy than rolls of Gamgee.

20

Horses are very sensitive to taste, which can lead to them refusing to drink water from a source different to the one they are used to. If travelling to a competition, take your own water supply with you in a large container: if this isn't practical (for example, if you are going to be away from home for several nights) add a little mint flavouring to the water at home to accustom the horse to it – and then add to drinking water as usual when stopping somewhere new, and it will disguise any unfamiliar taste. **Tip:** Many horses travelling long distances will refuse to drink whilst in transit and may become dehydrated. They may be quite happy to nibble at food, however, so supply a well-soaked haynet, which will ensure they have some liquid intake.

21

Lengths of guttering cut to size and lined with insulating material make neat coverings for exposed water pipes around the yard and ensure that the lagging doesn't get waterlogged, tatty, or chewed by horses and rodents.

22

Use an old elasticated cot sheet over your wheelbarrow when taking it to the muck heap – it will help stop any bedding blowing away or falling out and making more work to do sweeping up afterwards.

23

Enter shows in plenty of time – not just to ensure that the classes you want to enter are not full, but because it's cheaper. Entries on the day usually cost more than those made in advance. **Tip**: Practise riding in your show jacket a few times before going to a show so that you don't feel stiff and awkward in it, which may affect your riding.

24

Wear one or even two pairs of nylon tights under your jodhpurs to help keep warm in cold weather – they won't change the fit of your jodhpurs too dramatically, and are very effective.

25

Wear popsocks or cut down nylon tights to make it easier to get tight-fitting long riding boots on and off.

26

A bag of frozen peas makes a cheap, simple and reusable emergency ice-pack.

27

Reduce wastage of hay and make it last longer with greedy horses by placing one haynet inside two or three others.

28

If your horse is too young to be freeze-marked, use a contrasting vegetable dye to mark your postcode on his coat, renewing it as necessary.

29

Wisping is an excellent way of improving muscle tone and helping to put a bloom on the coat – instead of buying a stuffed pad, make a traditional wisp by twisting a rope of hay. They are

How to make a hay wisp.

easy to make, cost next to nothing, are a way of using up instead of wasting left-overs from the barn floor, and last a surprisingly long time.

30

Horses as well as their riders can suffer from pre-competition nerves and anxiety: Bach Flower Rescue Remedy is worth trying for both humans and equines.

31

Save time cleaning out the back of your car if you have to transport bedding and hay in it by laying an old bed sheet inside, which can be lifted and shaken out later.

32

Some horses can become irritated by the addition of a lump of rock salt or a large stone to their feeds to prevent them bolting it. If this happens, add chaff instead, as each mouthful will have to be chewed more thoroughly before it can be swallowed. Another effective way of preventing a horse from bolting his feed is to sweep clear an area of his stable floor, and then spread the feed across this, preventing him from taking large mouthfuls.

33

In very icy weather, or when snow has settled on the ground, muck out directly onto the yard (removing the droppings first). When it freezes again, it will create a rough surface which horses and handlers are less likely to slip on.

34

Fill a couple of dustbins with water during cold spells and leave close to the stable and the field trough. These will give you a plentiful supply of water close to hand if the pipes freeze.

35

Soaking hay can be a problem during freezing weather – steaming it may be a better alternative. Place either loose hay or a filled haynet inside a sturdy plastic bag (such as the sort shavings are packed in) and then pour over it one or two kettlesful of water which has just boiled. Tie the neck firmly with a piece of baler twine and leave until cool before feeding. Alternatively place the hay inside a dustbin, add hot water as before and then place the lid on top. **Tip:** Make sure hay is shaken out, not left in slices, otherwise the steam from the hot water may not penetrate through to the centre.

36

Don't rip open shavings bales – open carefully at one end so the bags are left intact. Sturdier than dustbin bags, they can be used for all sorts of things, from collecting baler twine in, storing loose hay sweepings from the ends of bales, transporting hay to fields without spilling, steaming hay in and even for storing rugs.

37

Stirrup leathers are much easier to remove and replace if you first tilt the saddle into a vertical position, with the pommel resting against a firm surface, such as a table. Press down on the cantle and you will find that the stirrup bars will stand slightly away from the tree, making it quick and easy to slide the stirrup leathers off and on.

38

When buying a show jacket, take along your body protector so you can try on the jacket over the top of it. This way you can ensure a good, comfortable fit, rather than having to guess whether it is right.

39

When using brushing boots with Velcro fastenings, take the added precaution of taping

over the tops with insulating tape for extra
security.

40

If pulling the tail of a difficult horse,
have an assistant hold the horse inside a stable
and drape the tail over the top of the lower door
whilst you are pulling so you are not in danger of
being kicked. Place a towel over the door first so
the sensitive skin under the tail is not damaged.

41

Make up your own water tray to practise
jumping over by removing all the fittings from an
old house door, and then painting it blue. By
cutting the door in half across its width, adding
feet and painting it, you can also make a set of
upright fillers.

42

If you have a young horse or one who
tends to be anxious about certain vehicles on the
roads, such as tractors or buses, ask your local
riding club if they would be interested in
organising a traffic training day when you and
other interested riders can work on solving these
problems in a safe environment with the help of an
instructor. By getting a group of people together,
the exercise becomes cheaper and more feasible to
set up. In addition to different vehicles, during
such sessions horses can also become accustomed
to other road hazards such as cones, rubbish bags
and signs.

43

If you tend to get saddle sore, use a seat saver on your saddle; they are also nice and snug to sit on during the cold winter months. You can make one cheaply and easily from an old fleecy or foam-filled numnah: wash it thoroughly first, then cut off the flaps and stitch along the raw edges. Attach a piece of elastic, which can be slipped beneath the saddle skirts, and two long tapes with Velcro at the ends, which can be fastened beneath the gullet to help keep it all secure.

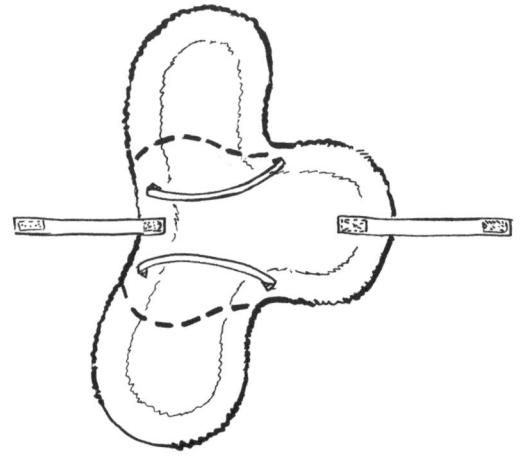

A seat saver is easy to make from an old fleecy numnah.

44

Save old plastic hypodermic syringes from veterinary visits – dispose of the used needles safely first. Smaller syringes can be useful for cleaning out deep and puncture wounds, and larger ones are handy for administering oral medicines such as cough mixtures.

45

If your horse is reluctant to take the bit when bridling him, try smearing the mouthpiece with honey, treacle, or even a little minty flavoured toothpaste. Do also make sure you don't bang his teeth with the bit, which will make him awkward. This can sometimes happen when unbridling too, particularly with a head-shy horse who may throw up his head, when the bit may not only bang against his front teeth, but actually become hooked over the lower ones, panicking him even more. This can be avoided by offering a titbit as you remove the bridle – he will lower his head and open his mouth for the food, allowing the bit to slide out without difficulty. **Tip:** If bridling up a tall horse who is not very co-operative and puts his head up in the air, to the point where you can't reach it with your hand, use the loop of the bridle headpiece to capture his nose and draw it downwards until you can put an arm around it.

46

Make your own horsey treats cheaply by drying slices of apple in a low-temperature oven. They will also be free of any additives!

47

Nettles are a good source of iron and can help put a bloom on the coat. Rather than buying an expensive supplement, harvest your own –

select the tops of young plants and allow to wilt for twenty-four hours to neutralise the sting – then chop up finely and add to feeds. **Tip**: Never collect nettles from roadsides, as they may be contaminated by vehicle exhaust fumes.

48

Instead of paying for herbal supplements, add herbs to your grazing and let your horse select for himself what he wants. As herbs are not always very competitive they can become stifled by grass growth and are also easily destroyed by spraying, but this difficulty can be solved by clearing a margin around the edge of the field where you can sow them. This will eliminate competition from other herbage, and you can avoid spraying the area; meanwhile the bulk of the grazing remains unaffected. Herbal seed mixes can be bought from agricultural seed merchants: useful herbs to include are ribgrass, chicory, yarrow, dandelion, and sheep's parsley, which are all palatable and rich in essential minerals.

49

Use a weigh tape to judge whether your horse is gaining or losing condition. Measure him each week, as your eye is not always the most reliable guide and you tend to notice only dramatic changes rather than more subtle ones.

50

Round off the corners of fields by nailing fencing rails diagonally across them. This will reduce the chances of a horse getting trapped in a corner and being bullied mercilessly by the others.

51

If you are planning to buy a horse, take a camcorder with you when going to view it. You can later view the tape at leisure to refresh your memory: and if you decide to buy will also have a record of all the vendor's replies to your questions so that should a problem arise later it will be easier to seek legal redress.

52

Replace cheap fittings on rugs with better quality ones – it may seem an unnecessary expense but they will be less likely to bend, break, damage straps or injure the horse, any of which incidents could prove not just downright inconvenient but very much more costly than replacing the fittings in the first place. **Tip:** Save the fittings from old rugs to keep as spares to help reduce repair costs.

53

The quickest and easiest way to clean leather riding gloves is whilst you are wearing them.

54

Remove leather straps from smart stable, summer and travelling rugs before washing as the dye used may bleed and end up discolouring the rug fabric. If you have to clean them frequently, replace the straps with more washing-friendly nylon ones.

55

Stick reflective patches onto your horse's turn-out rug so you can easily spot him when you go out to catch him in the field on winter days when it grows dark early. Adhesive dots and strips can be bought separately or you could cut up old reflective tabards and leg bands no longer in good enough condition to wear, and glue or stitch them on. If several horses are sharing grazing, arrange the patches in different patterns so you can distinguish between them easily and not waste time catching the wrong one.

Reflective patches on your horse's rug can help you spot him in the dark!

56

Try running a secondhand clothing and equipment sale – you will raise some cash from your unwanted bits and pieces and can pick up bargains from other vendors. Ordinary secondhand sales are worth checking out too as they are often a good source of cheap but perfectly robust and functional equipment such as buckets, storage containers and brooms.

57

Don't throw old broom heads away – even though they may be a bit tatty they can be used to make a handy mud remover for boots.

58

Make sure annual 'booster' vaccinations are kept up to date both for the good of your horse's health and because you may be refused entry at a show if it has lapsed (even if only by as little as a day). If the whole course has to be started over again, it will also be more expensive than keeping booster shots up to date.

59

If you feel your horse would benefit from a different type of bit, try using a bit hire service – many saddlers offer one or you can find mail-order services advertised in equestrian magazines. This will give you the chance to try out different bits without the expense of having to buy them, until you find the right one which both you and your horse are happy with. **Tip:** Always try out a new bit in a safe environment before going out for a hack or competing with it.

60

New leather boots can sometimes rub and cause blisters – try using plastic bubble-wrap packaging in the problem areas, placing it inside your socks so it doesn't slip.

61

If you tend to get saddle sore but cannot use a seat saver (in competitions for example) try wearing a pair of padded Lycra cyclist's pants beneath your jodhpurs.

62

When trying out a new bridle for size, don't buckle it up – thread all the straps through their keepers instead to avoid damaging the leather: if it doesn't fit it can then be returned as new, without any quibble. When trying out a saddle, place a piece of thin, clean material beneath it (such as a tea-towel, or section of old bed sheet): this will be thin enough to allow you to judge the fit but will prevent the saddle lining from getting dirty or greasy.

63

Haynets can be awkward to fill if you don't have a helper to hold the top of the net open for you. Make wrestling with unco-operative haynets a thing of the past by screwing two sturdy hooks into the wall of your hay storage area at a distance of 24ins (60cm) apart and approximately 36ins (90cm) high. Then simply hang your haynet between the two hooks: use one hand to hold the front edge open, and you'll still have one hand free to stuff the hay in.

64

Removing the fillet strings from rugs can be a really unpleasant task if your horse tends to soil them – and difficult too if the knots have pulled tight. Sew a pair of metal D-rings to the back of the rug instead, and then sew a small trigger clip onto each end of the fillet string: these can then be clipped onto the metal D's, making the job much easier.

65

Bristles on yard brooms wear more on the front edge than the back: rather than throwing them away when this happens, extend their life for a little longer by removing the head and reversing it, so that the back edge becomes the new front edge. **Tip:** Buying yard brushes with replaceable heads is also cheaper than buying those with integral handles – when the bristles do finally wear out, you only have to replace the new head, and won't be paying extra for the handle too.

66

If the noise made by aerosol, or even pump-action type bottles makes your horse anxious when applying fly repellents, try squirting a little onto a body brush or soft cloth instead and wiping it over his coat. **Tip:** Fly repellents may need to be reapplied every couple of hours for maximum effectiveness, which can be a problem if you are planning a long ride. Make your own fly wipes by spraying repellent onto several squares of cloth, and then placing them in a plastic bag, securing the neck with a metal tie so that the repellent doesn't all evaporate, and the wipes remain damp. The bag can then be slipped into a pocket or bum bag when you go out for a long ride, enabling you to renew your horse's fly protection whenever necessary by wiping the impregnated material over his coat.

67
Save suitable vegetable and fruit peelings – such as from carrots, parsnips, turnips, cabbage and apples – when preparing your own meals to add interest to your horse's feeds.

68
A single action apple corer and slicer costs very little to buy but makes slicing apples into fingers ready to add to feeds quicker, easier, and safer than using a knife. Knives are also more likely to be 'borrowed' for cutting strings on hay and straw bales by other people – who then often forget to return them afterwards!

69
Rather than buying expensive deodorisers for your stable, once you have put the

bed up against the walls, try sprinkling
bicarbonate of soda on the floor instead to help kill
smells effectively: it is inexpensive and easy to
obtain.

70

A wide range of plastic boxes with snap-
on lids can be bought very cheaply from hardware
stores and markets and are ideal for keeping
bandages and first-aid kits in – and are cheaper
than buying purpose made boxes from equestrian
retail outlets.

71

If you use a metal wheelbarrow and find
that the tray rusts away before chassis, don't
throw the chassis away. Cut a large plastic oil
drum in half lengthways and bolt it to the chassis
to form a new tray.

*A plastic oil drum can be put to good use to make a
wheelbarrow tray.*

72

When walking a cross-country course, take a notepad and pen so you can jot down notes to help jog your memory about the route and ways to tackle certain fences. If you are competing in a show-jumping class, walk the jump-off course after you have walked and memorised the first-round course, noting all the turns and approaches where you can save time.

73

Lay old carpeting in those areas of your horse's field which tend to get a lot of wear and tear – such as gateways and around water-troughs and hay racks. This will help prevent the ground from getting too badly poached during the winter months, which may discourage horses from drinking. Rubber- or foam-backed carpet works best. **Tip**: It is best to lay the carpeting down before the ground becomes too wet.

74

When bringing a horse in from the field in the dark, it isn't always practical or safe to try and lead the horse, open and shut gateways and hold a torch all at the same time. Solve the problem by clipping a front bicycle lamp onto your belt.

75

Don't throw away old cooking fat from the kitchen – save it to grease the soles of the hooves to help prevent snow and ice building up in winter. Leave a pot with a paintbrush handy by the stable door so it is easy to do before turning out in the field.

76

Discourage crib biters from chewing the tops of stable doors by securely nailing a couple of stiff bristled broomheads to them. **Tip:** Stable vices such as crib biting often start as a result of boredom and/or hunger: make sure your horse has adequate exercise, turn him out for as long as possible each day and when he has to be stabled, ensure he has sufficient hay to keep him occupied.

77

When clipping, the hairs have a habit of getting everywhere, and can be itchy at best and painful if they actually penetrate the skin or get in your eyes. If your overalls do not have elasticated cuffs, slip a rubber band over them at the wrists. Keep clipped hairs out of your eyes by wearing an eye visor – available from DIY shops – and avoid inhaling them by wearing a dust mask, also from DIY stores.

78

On very cold nights your horse's water bucket may freeze over, resulting in him going thirsty. Help to prevent this by bedding the bucket inside a larger one or a cardboard box filled with hay – use old sweepings from the hay area which cannot be fed and which would otherwise be thrown away and wasted.

79

Look out for ads in local papers – or enquire at shops – for secondhand dress rails: they make excellent rug racks which can be easily moved to one side out of the way in the tackroom, or wheeled out of doors to dry wet rugs.

80

Rug fronts often suffer when horses browse in hedgerows or over fencing. Ask your saddler to stitch in a chrome leather apron over the chest area to prolong the life of the rug and save on future rug repairs.

81

Sharp teeth can quickly make the cheeks and tongue sore, causing riding problems; also as food will not be chewed properly it can also lead to poor digestion and bigger feed bills as a result. Ask your vet to check and rasp your horse's teeth annually (twice a year if he is old) to ensure this doesn't happen. Add a handful of salt to your horse's water bucket after rasping, as this will then act as an antiseptic mouthwash each time he takes a drink. **Tip:** A salt water solution is also a cheap and effective antiseptic wash for bathing cuts and injuries.

82

If your horse has sensitive skin or is clipped, a plastic kitchen pan scourer makes easy work of removing dried mud and sweat from his coat without tears – and is also very cheap to buy.

83

Learn dressage tests by drawing out a plan of the arena and then 'riding' through it with your fingers at the appropriate markers. This is an easy and effective way of learning tests without riding them endlessly on your horse, risking him becoming bored or anticipating the movements.

Tip: Keep your old dressage score sheets, and the next time you ride the same test you will be able to look back and find out which movements particularly need to be worked on to help improve your score.

84

Keep a supply of homoeopathic remedies for first-aid purposes. If stored correctly they will last almost indefinitely, unlike many 'orthodox' drugs which have a limited shelf-life, and are therefore more economical, as well as being effective. Homoeopathic remedies can also be used safely on competition horses as they do not contain prohibited substances.

85

Prevent sugar-beet from freezing in the winter by soaking it in an insulated picnic-type cool-box.

86

Get together with other owners at the yard to share vets' visits for routine vaccinations and tooth rasping – it will cut the cost of travelling charges. This often applies to farriers too.

87

Get maximum value – and benefit – from lessons by asking someone to video you. Later you can replay it and will be better able to appreciate the instructor's corrections – and if you watch it again before your next schooling session it will act as a reminder for all the points you need to concentrate on.

Spot your mistakes – and your good points – by asking a friend to video your schooling sessions.

88

In small paddocks, use a portable knapsack sprayer to spot-treat weeds – a little goes a long way and it saves money on both chemicals and having to hire a contractor. **Tip:** Always follow the manufacturer's advice about how long to leave grazing before re-introducing horses after spraying.

89

Big bales of straw are now becoming more common, and small, more easily managed bales harder to obtain and often more expensive to buy. Transferring slices of straw from big bales to the stable can be awkward, however, as they are too large to fit into a wheelbarrow. The special barrows designed to carry big bales are ideal, but expensive to buy and not necessarily practical if you are in a small yard, or where access to the stables is narrow. The answer is to make a sheet to carry it in, similar to the muck sheets used in racing yards: either cut down a piece of tarpaulin, or an old bed sheet to around 4ft (1.2m) square, and attach a handle to each corner. Several slices can then be placed on top of it and the handles used to gather up the corners of the sheet and carry it to the stable with the minimum of mess and bother.

90

It's cheaper to buy oil for feeding purposes in bulk, but it is awkward lifting and accurately measuring it out of large containers. Using a funnel, decant it into a clean plastic container with a push-down pump dispenser (available from farm shops, or save old shampoo and liquid soap dispensers with these types of tops) – this will deliver the oil without mess and quickly and easily.

32

91

Make a cheap anti-weaving grid by screwing an upright of wood to the centre of the lower stable door.

Simple anti-weaving device.

92

Cleaning out guttering is time-consuming and may be costly if much debris has been flushed down the downpipe and clogged up the drainage system. You can buy mesh grids to fit – or you can make your own out of chicken wire. Cut strips which are slightly wider than the gutter diameter, curve them slightly along their length and then lie them in the guttering. When you want to clean out the gutters, all you have to do is lift up each length, shake the leaves off and then replace it.

93

Make a checklist with everything on it that you need for a show, to ensure that you don't arrive only to find you have left a vital piece of equipment at home. Tick everything off as you load it. **Tip:** Laminate the list (large stationery and office suppliers often offer this service) to help extend its life, and then use a wax pencil to tick off items when packing them. After the show you can then wipe off the ticks with a soft damp cloth and use the list again and again for future outings rather than having to make a new one for every trip.

Remember to load the horse!

94

When cleaning your grooming kit, use a horse shampoo to wash brushes rather than household detergent which may irritate the skin.

95

To help work shampoo into the horse's coat and thoroughly clean scurf and dirt from the roots, work up a lather and then use a rubber curry comb to massage it into the hair using circular movements. **Tip:** If your horse is frightened of hosepipes use a watering-can instead when giving him a bath.

96

Stop hay from blowing away or being trampled into the mud out in fields by placing it inside large 'muck bucket' plastic containers, secured to fence posts (uprights not horizontal rails) at intervals. Punch holes through the bottom of the containers to prevent them filling with rain water.

97

Up to eighty per cent of a horse's feed energy may be used to keep him warm – rugging him up well ensures that you are not spending more on feed than is necessary. Rather than buying several different weights of stable rug, adding a liner or blanket to a lightweight rug will make it suitable for really chilly weather, and it is easy to adjust the warmth factor with changes in the weather.

98

Sew extra pockets onto an old kitchen apron: slip scissors, thread, comb and plait bands into the pockets so they are easily to hand when plaiting up for a show. Push a few pre-threaded needles through the fabric ready for use.

99

Make simple saddlebags by sewing a couple of pockets onto the sides of a saddlecloth to pop sandwiches and a collapsible hoofpick into if you are planning a long picnic ride. Use Velcro tape to secure the pocket flaps to ensure you don't lose your lunch when enjoying a quick canter!

100

A chamois leather, lightly dampened, is soft to use on the head when grooming, and for removing dust and grease from an area where you cannot groom briskly with a brush. A dampened and well-wrung-out chamois leather can also be placed beneath the saddle to reduce the likelihood of it slipping.

101

Try adding a tablespoonful of cider vinegar (organic is best) to feeds each day to help horses who are growing older and beginning to show signs of stiffness and arthritis. **Tip:** Arthritic horses stiffen up quickly when stabled overnight in cold weather as they tend to move around less in the confined space. Encourage more mobility by dividing the evening hay into three rations and placing each in different corners of the box, and placing his water in the fourth so he has to move around a little.

102

Human Tubigrip bandages are a quick and easy way of keeping poultices and dressings in place on legs and feet. To put on a foot, slide the Tubigrip on to just above the fetlock joint. Place the poultice in position over the sole, with a piece of plastic over the top, then pull the Tubigrip down over the poultice, twist and pull back up over the hoof to make a double thickness. This will hold it in place whilst you then finally secure it by bandaging and/or a poultice boot.

STEP 1

STEP 2

STEP 3

Securing a poultice or dressing using a Tubigrip bandage.

103

Lifting a soaked haynet out of water to drain is heavy work: make it easier by fixing a metal ring to the wall with a sturdy nail below it. When the hay has soaked for long enough, thread the drawstring of the net through the ring above and use it as a pulley to lift the net up: once out of the water, hook the end of the drawstring over the nail to secure it.

Make light work of lifting heavy soaked haynets with this simple pulley arrangement.

104

Stick an 'L' plate onto the front and back of a tabard when out riding on the roads – it is a sign that is instantly understood by all motorists, and more effective than a printed message.

105

Place a folded towel across your horse's forehead when bathing him to prevent water and shampoo getting in his eyes. Tuck each end firmly under the sides of the headcollar to keep it in place.

106

Prevent your hands from slipping on the reins in wet weather by using rubber-covered reins and gloves with rubber pimples on the palms.

107

Don't be miserly with bedding – it is a false economy and you will end up throwing far more away. A deep bed is not only less wasteful but offers better protection from scrapes on the stable flooring, and is more likely to encourage your horse to lie down when resting.

108

If your horse is frightened by clippers, even if you don't have your own set you can still spend some time getting him used to the idea. Start by running a hand-held car vacuum-cleaner near his stable, progress to running it inside the stable once he has grown accustomed to it, and gradually move closer with it until you can run it all over his body.

109

If your horse has a back problem, check your horse's rugs as well as the fit of his saddle – they are often overlooked but are frequently a major source of such problems, and if not a good fit will certainly contribute to any existing discomfort.

110

When finishing off a hand-pulled mane, use rubber thimbles, washing-up or rubber surgical gloves to give your fingers a better grip on the hairs and prevent blisters.

111

When handling nervous horses, scratch the neck and along the crest with your fingertips rather than giving hearty pats: the horse will find the action far more soothing and less aggressive.

112

Top up water buckets with a kettleful of hot water in the winter – if you don't have a kettle on the yard, take a Thermos flask of hot water with you instead. This will not only delay it freezing over, but will encourage your horse to drink – many will reduce their intake if the water is too cold, and may suffer dehydration as a result.

40

113

Not all oral medicines and wormers are palatable, making it difficult to administer them to some horses, or to be sure they have received the correct dosage. Try mixing granules and powders with treacle or honey, which can then be smeared onto the horse's tongue with a narrow wooden or plastic spatula – it will not only taste pleasant but be impossible for him to spit out again. If the horse is difficult to handle in this way, mix the medicine into the treacle or honey as before, but make it into a sandwich with a piece of bread instead. This can also be done with paste wormers normally administered with a syringe, if the horse is unco-operative.

There are many ways to make wormers and medicines more palatable – try serving up a wormer sandwich, for example!

114

Stable bandages can provide extra warmth in cold weather – the equivalent of adding an extra blanket – and are useful if a horse is old, or ill and weak, when you may not want to put extra weight on his back.

115

You don't need a lot of jumps in order to be able to practise your course-riding techniques. Using just three fences, build a Y-shaped grid of jumps which can be continuously jumped in either direction – you can make turns wide and easy, or tighter to practise jump-off tactics.

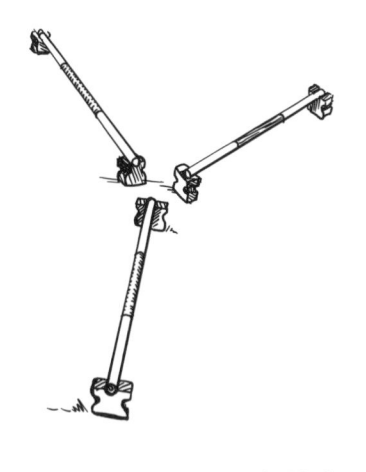

Just three fences, arranged in a simple Y-shaped grid, allow for variety in jumping practice sessions.

116

Horse hairs (and those from other animals) which become stuck to your show jacket are easy to remove with a rubber washing-up glove – pop it on, dampen it slightly and 'brush' the fabric briskly with your hand. The hairs will stick to the glove: rinse them off frequently in a bowl of warm water. **Tip:** It is easiest to do this whilst the jacket is being worn.

117

Before turning a new horse out in the field with others, first take it for a ride with the most dominant horses to give them a chance to get safely acquainted, and reduce the likelihood of the newcomer being bullied.

118

Sugar-beet tea is a useful pick-me-up after hard work or a competition. Make it by soaking your sugar-beet as normal, but with double the usual amount of water. Once it has finished soaking, drain off the beet using a colander or sieve and offer it as a refreshing, tasty and energy-giving drink.

119

A really quick and easy way to clean out all the green scummy bits from the sides of a field water-trough is to take a piece of nylon garden netting, scrunch it up into a large ball and use it as a giant scourer.

120

As a special treat for your horse, you might like to try making him a cake. Mix together 15 cups of coarse mix, 2 jars of molasses, 3 cups of sugar-beet tea and 5 cups of plain flour. Press into a spring-form cake tin and bake in an oven at 180°C until dark brown and firm to the touch – around 25 minutes. Crumble pieces off to give to your horse as a special birthday or Christmas treat.

121

Rubber car-floor mats make good draught excluders: cut in half and nail to the bottom edge of stable doors, then screw (not nail) a thin lath of wood over the top to secure. Old mats can be picked up for next to nothing at secondhand sales and from scrap yards – or you may be replacing your own.

122

Dangerously sharp edges are exposed on metal salt and mineral block holders as the block wears down: some horses will also crunch their way through these licks at an alarmingly expensive rate. Try buying cylindrical rather than brick-shaped blocks, which have a hole through the centre instead: thread a piece of stout rope or plaited baler twine through the hole and hang up so that it swings freely, and it will not only be safer but prevent wastage and provide some entertainment as a toy into the bargain.

Cylindrical salt-lick suspended on a rope

123

Instead of buying an expensive pre-printed log book or equine Filofax in which to keep the details of your horse, make your own. Ring binders make sturdy covers and can be bought for just a few pence at secondhand sales. It is easy to add additional information and details – and there are no problems of running out of space. The binder can be handed on to a new owner if you sell the horse at a future date, and can provide an invaluable record of his history. Keep details not just of veterinary treatments, but shoeing, worming, feeding, useful telephone numbers and competition successes. **Tip:** Keep portrait photographs of your horse in your folder, ideally taken from both sides plus front and rear views. In the event of him being stolen these can help to make identification and recovery easier. Make sure your photographs are kept up to date, bearing in mind that his appearance can change dramatically from one season to the next.

124

Mucking-out equipment is expensive to replace, so it makes sense to store it correctly. Keep brushes and forks under cover where the handles will not become rotted by rain, and avoid leaning on broom handles if you stop for a chat as this will bend and damage the bristles. Prolong the working life of wheelbarrows by standing them up-ended when not in use, otherwise rain water will collect in the pan and rust it.

125

If you get a puncture in your wheelbarrow tyre, you can effect an instant repair using an aerosol tyre foam: one aerosol will mend many punctures.

126

Clipper oil can occasionally cause irritation and blistering on sensitive skins: so keep a cloth handy (an old tea-towel is ideal) for wiping off excess oil each time you lubricate the blades and before recommencing clipping. **Tip:** Brush off loose hairs after clipping so they do not become stuck to rug linings causing irritation: then wipe over the clipped areas with a damp sponge to remove any last small traces of clipper oil from the coat.

127

Keep hairy legs and heels trimmed up in winter as this will make it quicker and easier to dry them, and in very severe freezing conditions the wet hair will not form uncomfortable little icicles around the fetlocks. Dense hair also tends to hold in moisture and creates warm damp conditions ideal for bacteria to thrive in, so may be more likely to lead to problems such as cracked heels and mud-fever. If feathering is kept trimmed these are less likely to occur, but if they do you will be more likely to spot the problem early, before it has become serious. **Tip:** When trimming up, leave just a small tuft of hair at the ergot to help channel water away from the heels.

128

A horse toy is cheaply made from a large plastic squash or milk carton. Remove and dispose of the cap, and then half fill with water, adding a few drops of peppermint essence to add an interesting smell. Loop a piece of plaited baler twine through the handle and hang up so that it can swing freely. Out in the field some horses will enjoy a football or plastic traffic cone to play with. Such toys may distract them from damaging other more valuable items such as fencing or trees.

129

A little baby oil brushed through the tail after washing it will help mud slide out of it during the winter, making it easier to care for without breaking or damaging the hairs.

130

After washing a tail, grasp the hairs just below the end of the tail bone and whiz them briskly round in a circle – this quickly gets rid of excess water, although it may soak anyone standing nearby!

'Spin-drying' the tail after washing.

131

Smear vegetable cooking oil onto your hands and rub over the horse's legs, belly and insides of the hind legs to help prevent mud from sticking during the winter – it will come off easily when dry. **Tip:** Apply the oil to the horse when it is clean and dry; do not put it on top of mud, or apply when wet, otherwise it will just sit on top and trap, rather than repel, moisture. Vaseline or baby oil can be used if preferred.

132

You will probably spend less time riding in winter than in summer and especially if you do have a particularly severe spell of weather which stops you riding altogether, take advantage of the opportunity to get jobs done such as saddle reflocking and vaccinations, which might normally interfere with your riding activities. Get them out of the way at a time when you can't ride anyway rather than lose out on riding time in the summer.

133

Security-mark saddlery with your postcode using metal stamps – you can either buy your own set, get together with friends to buy a set between you, or cheaper still, take your tack down to your local police station who will do it for you.

134

To help lift grease from the coats of clipped horses and help keep infection at bay pour hot water into a bucket (test that it is not scalding

– it should be no hotter than you can bear it on your own skin) and add a few drops of lavender or tea tree essential oil. Dunk a clean towel into the water, and then wring it out so it is just damp and rub firmly over the coat in a circular motion, rinsing and squeezing out again after each couple of circles.

135

Haynets often swing round as the horse eats, ending up in a tightly twisted drawstring which is difficult to remove quickly and easily. Fit a sturdy, almost closed hook (the type with a blunt hook end) from which you can hang your net as usual. When you want to remove it, simply slip the drawstring upwards over the end of the hook.

Hang your haynet from a blunt, almost-closed hook and it will be easy to remove, no matter how twisted the drawstring.

136

Use an old colander to clear out debris from field water-troughs. During the winter it is also a good way of removing chunks of ice after you have broken them up.

137

Use a colander or mesh sieve to scoop out soaked sugar-beet and add to concentrate feeds. Any remaining liquid can then be sprinkled over hay to entice fussy feeders, or given simply as a treat. **Tip:** Coarse mixes are also good for encouraging fussy feeders to eat up as they are molassed and more tempting.

138

Hedgerows and field margins should be checked regularly for poisonous plants, which often thrive in such habitats. Unless you are an expert botanist they aren't always easy to identify, so take a pocket field book with you which shows the plants in their various stages of growth.
Tip: Improve your grazing by cutting back rough patches of grass: if it is a small area you can do this either with a strimmer or a ride-on lawnmower – remember to pick up the cuttings. This will increase the grazing area the horse will utilise and stops young growth from being choked.

139

Cut plastic oil drums in half lengthways to form fillers for show jumps or cross-country jumps to practise over: they are light and easy to

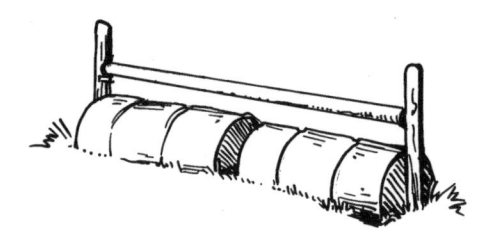

Plastic oil drums cut in half lengthways make useful jump fillers.

move around, won't rot or rust, and placed with the cut edges on the ground are also safe as they will not roll.

140

Cut a large plastic oil drum in half lengthways to make a cheap water-trough or hayrack for the field: they are also ideal containers if you have to soak several haynets at the same time. Wedge them into position with heavy scrap timber or half sleepers to prevent them rolling over.

141

Save the plastic sterile covers in which large syringes are packed – they make a useful receptacle for your hoof-oil brush, which will mean that everything else in your grooming kit won't get oily.

142

Cigarette filter tips (available from tobacconists) are handy for plugging stud-holes in shoes.

143

Alleviate the discomfort caused by cutting teeth in young horses by rubbing a little Bonjela or one of the other similar preparations used for children when teething, into the gums.

144

Make a fly net if your horse is prone to eye infections from summer flies and a fly fringe doesn't provide sufficient protection. Use netting from vegetable or fruit bags, or a piece of window curtain netting. Sew poppers or Velcro tape along the edges so that it can be wrapped around the cheekpieces of the headcollar, and to enable it to be easily removed when not required, and then add two lengths of plain tape or ribbon to the top corners. Punch two holes in the headcollar headpiece, one on either side, and slightly above the height of the eyes. (To gauge where the holes should go, mark their positions with a pen whilst the headcollar is on your horse.) The tapes are then threaded through these holes to ensure that the net doesn't slip down.

If your horse is bothered by summer flies, why not make him a fly net?

145

When trotting up a horse to determine lameness, make sure you don't hold the lead rope so taut as to restrict the head carriage – its movement may be an indicator as to which leg the horse is lame on. Remember also to turn the horse away from you, rather than towards you, so don't block the view of the observer – it's safer, too, as your toes won't get trodden on.

146

If your horse finds mane pulling uncomfortable, try rubbing a little oil of cloves into the neck at the base of the mane first – wear rubber gloves when applying it so that your own fingers don't go numb.

147

Nose nets can help in some cases of headshaking brought on by pollen allergies by acting as a crude filter. They are simple to make, using the toe end from one leg of a pair of tights or stockings. Having trimmed it to the right length and slid it over the muzzle, the remaining top end of the leg can be used to fashion soft ties with which to attach it to the bridle noseband to keep it in place.

148

Full-length waxed jackets are brilliant for riding in wet weather but the internal leg straps which hold the coat close to your legs can sometimes cause problems when dismounting –

the one on your right leg can occasionally get caught on the cantle of the saddle. Overcome this by replacing the buckle with a Velcro fastening which will come undone if this happens.

149

If you have to put hay out in the field in winter in a haynet and there is nowhere more suitable to hang it than the field fencing, ensure that when it is empty the net will not dangle dangerously low where feet may become entangled in it. This can be done by tying the drawstring to the fence as usual, then tie a second string to the bottom of the net and thread this length through net holes and around the horizontal rail so that the net lies along its length rather than hanging vertically from it.

If you have to use a fence on which to hang a winter haynet, secure the haynet as described above.

150

A scarf is warm in winter but is potentially dangerous when riding or when working around the yard – the ends can drop down when bending over. Wear a snood instead – it can be either pushed down around your neck or pulled up to keep your ears and head snug and cosy.

151

Should your horse be difficult about having his head clipped, try doing a bridle clip instead. Slip on the bridle to act as a guideline, and clip the lower half of the head up as far as the cheekpieces on each side: most horses will accept this more readily and it looks smarter than leaving the whole head unclipped.

152

The keepers of Fulmer snaffles often have a habit of going missing: if you lose one and don't have a spare, temporarily make do with an elasticated hair band – slip over the billet of the bridle cheekpiece, then twist tightly until just enough slack is left to slip over the end of the bit cheek and hold it in place.

153

Use a pair of battery-operated dog trimming clippers for clipping heads – the hair is finer on the face so it doesn't matter if the motor is less powerful, and it is a comparatively small area anyway. They are also generally very much quieter and with less vibration, so the horse is less likely to object to them, and as the blades are narrower it is easier to work around all the little fiddly areas.

154

The easiest and quickest way to roll a bandage is to lay the tape end against your thigh and then roll downwards, using your thigh as a support. This also ensures you have a firm rather than loose, and fairly consistent, pressure as you roll, which will make it easier to put on correctly tensioned bandages later. **Tip**: Make sure you lay tapes to the inside of the bandage as you roll, so that when you bandage your horse later they will end be on the right side.

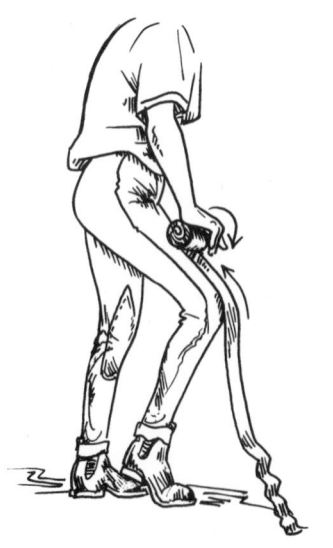

A neat and quick way to roll tail bandages.

155

Save old stirrup leathers rather than throwing them out: they may still make good neck-straps.

156

It is not ideal to leave a headcollar on your horse whilst he is out in the field as it makes it easier for thieves to catch him and there is a danger that he could get caught up on fencing. However, sometimes it is a necessary evil – with horses who are difficult to catch there may be no choice, or if you need to use a fly fringe or noseguard. In this case minimise the risk by using a lightweight leather headcollar, which unlike nylon will snap if he does accidentally get caught up.

157

Putting on a tail bandage is easier if you stand close and to one side of your horse's quarters, and rest the tail bone over the top of your shoulder – your horse cannot then clamp his tail down and you have two hands free to bandage with.

158

Rodent control can be a problem around yards: traps aren't always very effective, and whilst poison is, it can pose a hazard to other animals and young children. Try a natural deterrent such as a yard cat or two, which will also provide company for stabled horses.

A noseguard attached to a headcollar can protect your horse's muzzle from sunburn.

159

Horses with white or pink muzzles often suffer from sunburn during the summer: using non-allergenic total sun blocks is effective but they need to be reapplied several times during the day for maximum effectiveness. This can be expensive, especially if you own more than one horse. An alternative is to make a noseguard to protect against the sun: simply make a rectangular flap of stout material and attach it to the noseband of the headcollar, using Velcro tapes.

160

Replace tie tapes on bandages with Velcro for quicker and easier bandaging: it is also safer as it won't be possible to over-tighten them, causing damage to the tendons and ligaments.
Tip: Bandages should always be additionally secured for safety – stitching is the traditional method, but time-consuming and fiddly, especially if the horse is fidgety. Using insulating tape is much easier.

58

161

Don't have rubber reins recovered more than twice: the saddler can't use the same stitch holes each time and as a result the leather will become weakened.

162

Lunge reins always seem to acquire knots in them which pull tight and are almost impossible to undo again. The easiest way to unravel them is to use a hoofpick to push into the knot and loosen it to the point where your fingers can tease it out and finish the job. Because the point of the hoofpick point is blunt, it will not cut into and damage the lunge rein.

163

If you have trouble keeping both reins the same length when riding, slip a brightly coloured elastic band over each rein at the same distance from the bit, so you can judge both accurately and instantly. **Tip:** When using two pairs of reins, have one thin pair, and the other thicker so that it is easy to tell the difference between them by feel and without having to look.

164

Stand on a stout box when plaiting, so that hairs are drawn upwards into the plait rather than out sideways – this will enable you to ensure that any shorter hairs are incorporated into the plait, and to get the plait tighter and neater, avoiding a saggy, untidy and amateurish appearance. **Tip:** Don't wash the mane or tail just before you want to plait or pull it as the hairs will be slippery and hard to hold. If you are going to a show, wash them a couple of days beforehand.

165

Cheaply convert a cavesson to a flash noseband by securely stitching a loop of nylon web around the noseband front: then slip a leather strap through this to act as the dropping part. It may not be smart enough for competition wear, but is quite adequate for schooling and other general riding purposes and is easy to remove again if you wish. Suitable leather flash straps can be picked up secondhand or from saddlers at less than the cost of a new noseband, and if you later decide you want to keep it like this, you can ask your saddler to stitch in a smarter looking leather loop to hold the strap.

166

When washing towels used for drying off horses, don't add fabric conditioner – it may make them feel softer and fluffier, but they will be less absorbent. When washing rugs and horse clothing, avoid biological soap powders, which may irritate the skin.

167

Pin a piece of fabric or tissue impregnated with fly repellent to the peak of your hat whilst riding, so that you as well as your horse can enjoy fly-free rides during the summer.

168

If you do not wish to remove the reins from your horse's bridle whilst lungeing, secure them out of way so they cannot not slip over his head or dangle down dangerously near his front legs, by twisting them round each other beneath his neck and then catching them up through the throatlash of either the bridle or cavesson.

Keep the reins out of the way when lungeing by catching them up via the throatlash, as described above.

169

After cleaning water-troughs, add a dash of minty mouthwash to freshen them up and camouflage the lingering scent or taste of any disinfectants used.

170

If your horse dislikes having his mane pulled, try pulling the hairs out in an upwards, rather than sideways, direction as this is less painful.

171

To prevent neatly rolled bandages from unravelling and getting in a tangle, slip an elastic band over each bandage.

172

Unless showing (when plaits should always be stitched in) plait up using elastic bands matching the colour of the mane for speed. They are also quicker and easier to take out again afterwards – especially if you wish to remove them for the jumping phases of a one-day event after completing the dressage section.

173

Stop bristles at the sides of dandy brushes becoming squashed and broken by tacking a piece of leather to either side where your fingers normally hold it.

Dandy brush protector.

174

If you normally feed a cool ration but find it doesn't give your horse enough energy, don't increase the quantity – it is cheaper to buy the next energy level up instead and feed the same amount. Feeding oil is also a cost-effective way of providing energy for horses; but bear in mind that it will make your horse fat if he is receiving more energy than he is using up. **Tip:** Fussy feeders may be put off by large meals, and these can result in poor and inefficient digestion anyway: using oil to increase the energy content of a feed ration enables you to decrease the size of feed in these cases.

175

If you want to add extra holes to nylon web headcollars using an ordinary hole puncher you'll find it difficult to do and the holes will tend to fray. Overcome the problem and save yourself the expense of splashing out on a proper hole-rivetting kit (which you probably won't need to use very often anyway) by selecting a nail of the same diameter as the hole you wish to make. Holding it securely in a pair of pliers, heat the nail until it is very hot and then poke a hole through the nylon strap with the hot point: the nail will go through easily, and the heat will seal the edges of the hole preventing fraying.

176

When first introducing a young horse to the bit, use either a rubber or rubber-covered bit initially so that it is less frightening for him if, despite your precautions, his teeth get banged by the mouthpiece. Alternatively, if you prefer to use a metal bit, wrap some Vetrap round the mouth-piece which will also cushion the teeth in the event of this accidentally happening, and which will also make the bit feel less cold in his mouth.

177

Help keep stored rugs and saddlery free from damp by placing them inside cotton pillowcases (which will 'breathe') and then popping them inside a bin liner with sachets of silica gel.

178

Small gaps in stables which let in draughts can be effectively and cheaply blocked with tightly rolled wads of shredded newspaper.

179

In the lid of a jam jar, pierce a hole large enough to take the handle of your hoof oil brush. Pour hoof oil into the jar, and you will have a neat integral brush and lid arrangement which will prevent the brush from being mislaid or the handle from getting covered in oil.

A jam jar fitted with a brush makes a handy hoof-oil dispenser.

180

Horses who have learned to remove their headcollars by rubbing them off over one ear can

Use an old stirrup leather to provide extra security for a headcollar.

be foiled by making a couple of cotton or nylon web loops, and slipping one over the headpiece and one over the throatlash. Cut down an old stirrup leather and buckle it snugly around the neck just behind the ears so that it forms a second throat piece, threading it first through the loops attached to the headcollar.

181

Store bales of hay off the ground to prevent it from becoming damp – you often have to pay for wooden pallets, but old car tyres will do the job just as well, and can be obtained either free or for next to nothing from garages and scrap yards.

182

Plait together three strips of nylon tights, stitch one end firmly to your New Zealand rug and sew a clip on to the other end to make tough but non-chafing leg straps.

183

When clipping, use a piece of baler twine to check that the height of your clip is the same on each side.

184

Old vegetable racks can make excellent shelving containers for tackroom items such as tack-cleaning kit and for odds and ends. If you want to keep them out of reach of small fingers or other animals on the yard you can easily hang them higher up on the walls, from nails.

185

If your horse tends to blow himself out whilst you are tightening the girth, feed him a handful of hay and then try again whilst he is still munching.

186

Place unrolled bandages inside an old pillowcase before putting in the washing machine to help prevent them knotting themselves around other items.

187

A smart, cheap and effective way of displaying your rosettes is to take a length of wide ribbon and stitch a curtain ring to one end: the rosettes can then be tied or pinned to the tail of ribbon: use the curtain ring to hang them up from a nail or hook screwed into the wall.

188

When cleaning machine-washable girths keep the buckle tongues in place and prevent them from becoming wedged in one of the holes of the washing-machine drum by using a piece of wire wrapped over them to secure them.

Before machine-washing girths, secure the buckle tongues with a piece of wire.

189

Pop metal bits and stirrup irons in the dishwasher – they'll come out looking brand new.

190

Dividing the mane into wide bunches and securing firmly with elastic bands close to the crest so that it stands upright makes it quicker and easier both to see what you are doing when clipping your horse's neck, and to clip close to the root line.

191

Save your old toothbrushes: they make ideal small brushes for getting into tight areas when cleaning out hairs clogging up clippers and clipper blades.

192

To keep your boots spotless before showing classes, slip a pair of long, fluffless socks over them so they don't get muddy or dirty whilst mounting – ask someone to slip them off once you are on board.

193

Use the rough side of an old pan scourer to quickly and easily remove dried saliva from bits and to restore a bright finish when cleaning them.

194

Keep a small nail, box of cocktail sticks or spent matchsticks handy in the tackroom, to remove soap and dirt from clogged-up holes in stirrup leathers and bridlework.

195

Here's a quick, clean and easy way of applying hoof oil just before a class at a show. Take an empty shoe-shine bottle with a foam applicator pad, wash it out thoroughly and when dry fill it with hoof oil. Press the foam pad onto a piece of paper a few times until the oil flows into it, then it's ready for use. Screw the top on firmly to ensure the pad stays moist.

196

If your horse learns how to untie himself by pulling at the knot of his lead rope, attach a longer rope than usual to his headcollar, thread it

through the normal tie ring, and then on to a
second ring set to the side where he can't reach it
and tie as usual, to a piece of breakable string.

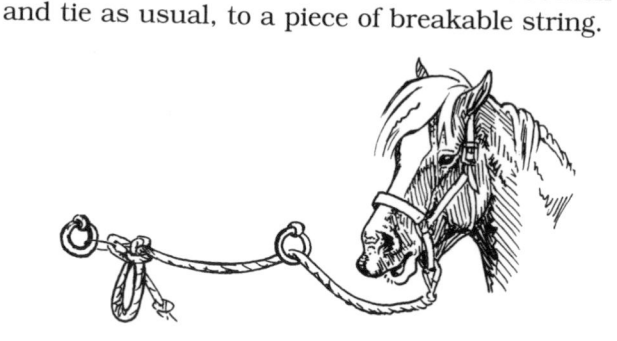

*Using two tie rings, as shown, may be the answer for an
'escape artist'.*

197

A small lock de-icer is cheap to buy,
lasts a long time and is small enough to fit easily
into a pocket – and is invaluable for de-icing frozen
field and yard padlocks in winter.

198

Use combination padlocks on field gates
and buildings if there are lots of people at the yard
– it's cheaper than having lots of keys cut and
there are no worries about losing keys.

199

Don't throw away old nail brushes: use
them for jobs such as scrubbing grease off synthetic
girths when hand washing them, and for removing
dirt from the soles and welts of riding boots.

200

Make your own clothing bib from an old bucket or even a discarded wellington boot. Cut the leg off the boots or the side out of the bucket and then trim to the right size and shape – it helps if you make a template first as a guide so that you don't make a mistake. On the top edge make three holes using a heated nail, and then tie a tape to each and attach to the centre and two side rings of the headcollar. It should sit snugly behind the chin and hang down just below the mouth. **Tip:** If using a bucket, be careful that the edges do not chafe – use insulating tape to line them.

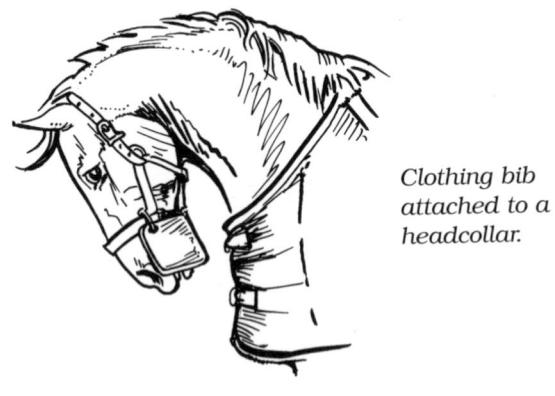

Clothing bib attached to a headcollar.

201

If your scrubbing brush has disappeared yet again and you don't have the time to search for it, a scrunched-up handful of dampened hay or straw makes an effective scourer to remove old feed from feed bins and slime from water containers.

Index